# the first summer study book for cello

### by cassia harvey

CHP188

©2007 by C. Harvey Publications All Rights Reserved.

www.charveypublications.com - print books
www.learnstrings.com - PDF downloadable books
www.harveystringarrangements.com - chamber music

# Cello Note Chart

## A string
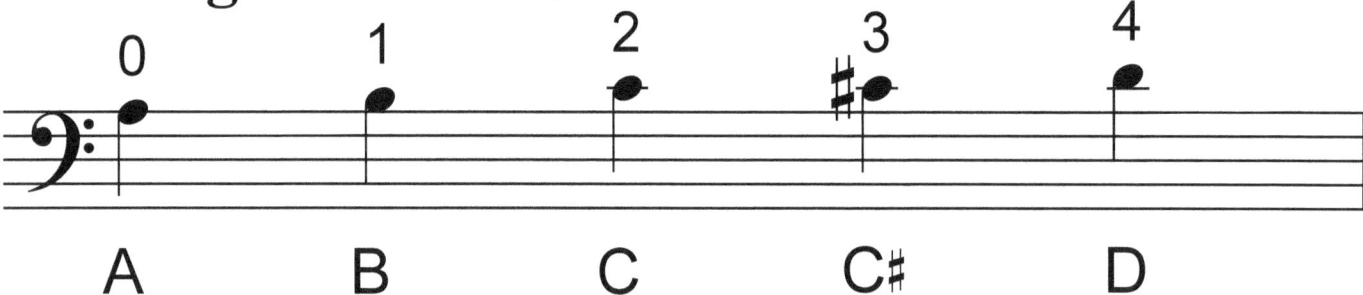

## D string
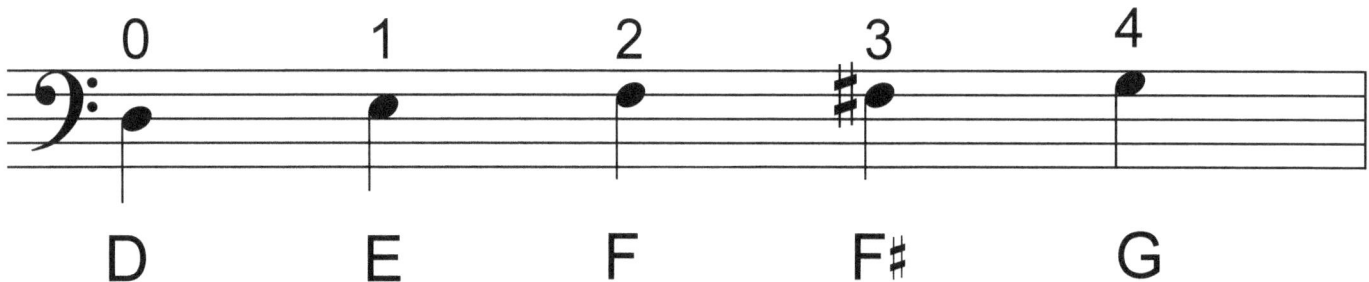

## G string
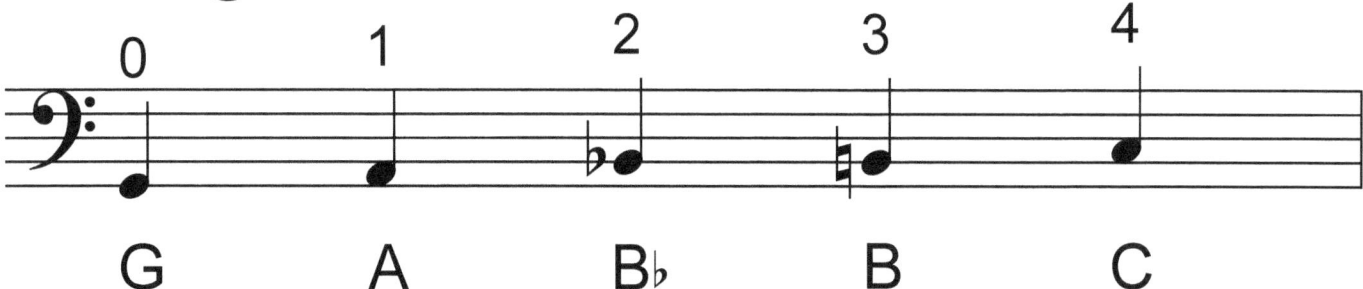

## C string
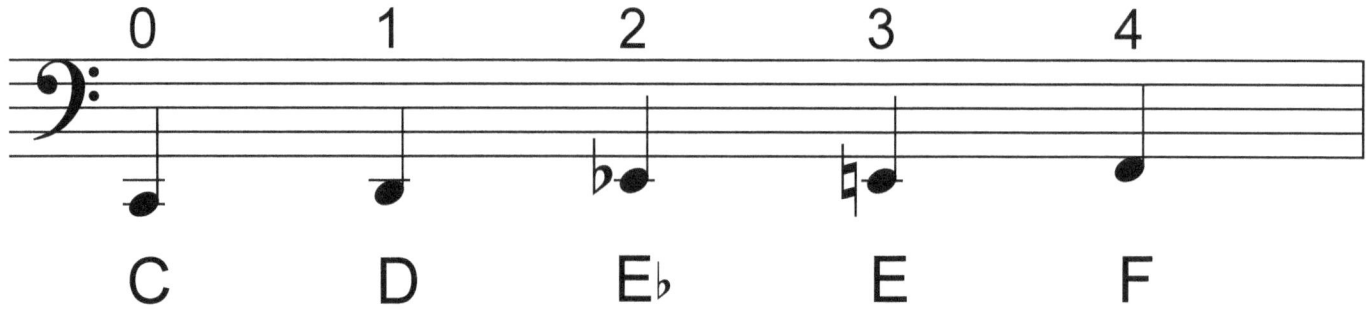

## 1. No more flimsy first fingers!

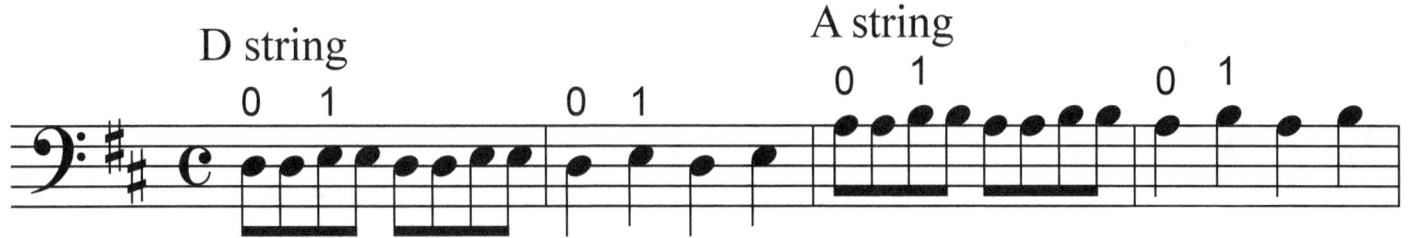

## 2. Cripple Creek

# 3. What Do You Do With a Drunken Sailor?

D string

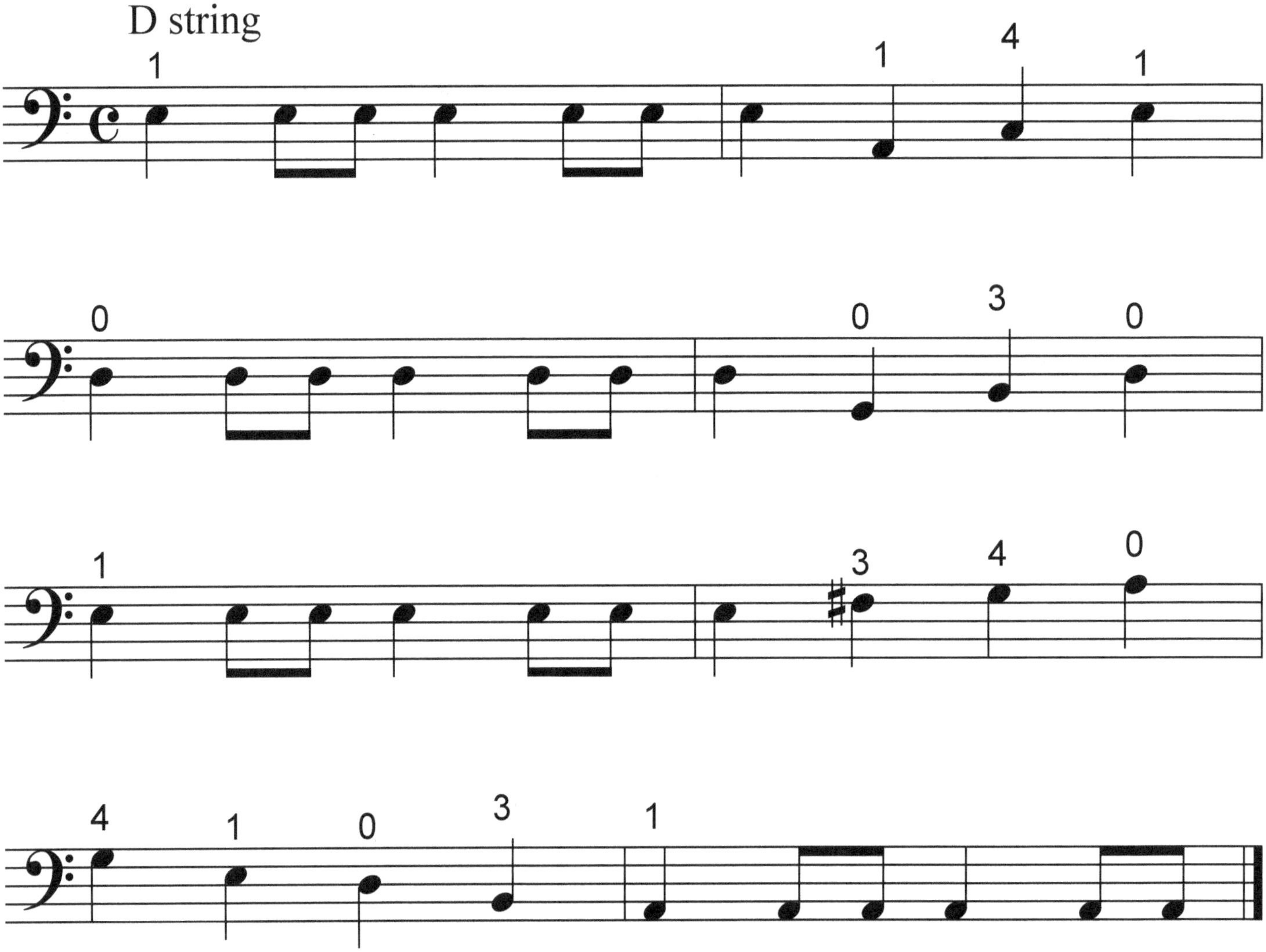

# 4. Drunken Sailor String Crossing

D string

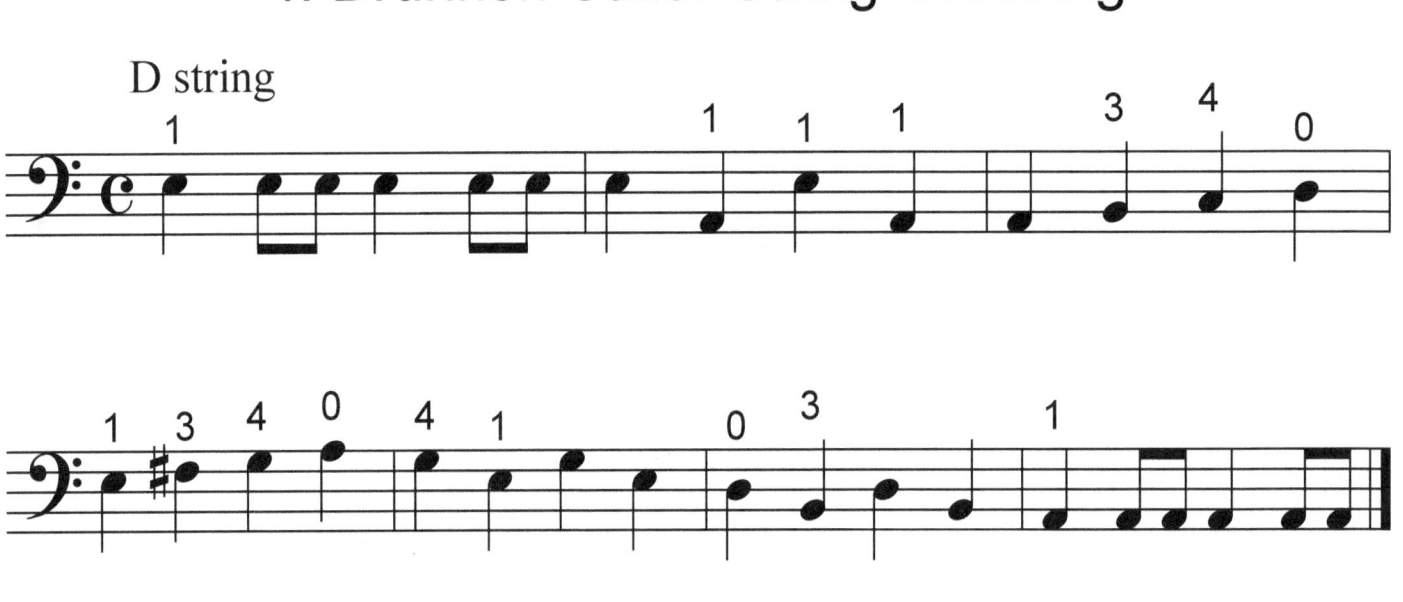

## 5. Fiddle Tune

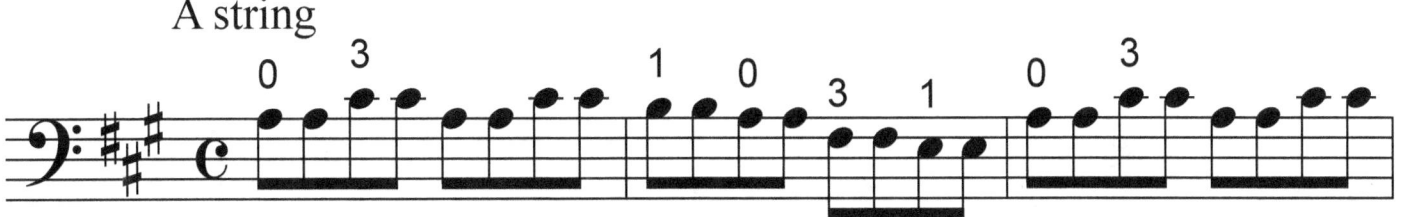
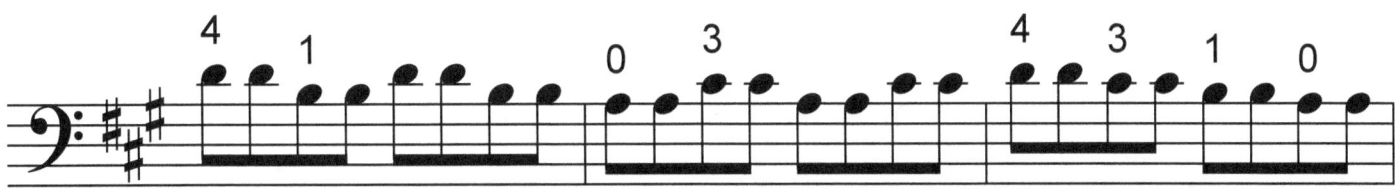
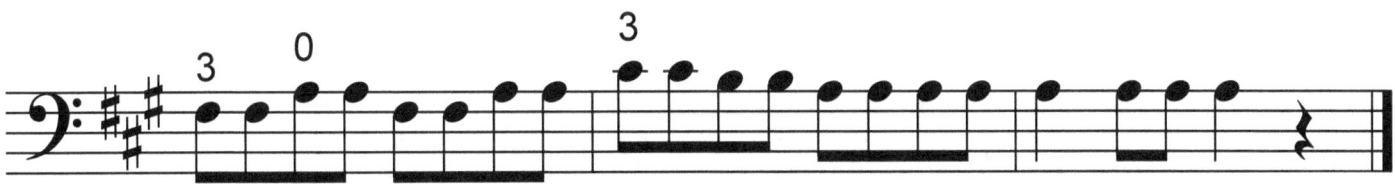

## 6. William Tell

©2007 C. Harvey Publications All Rights Reserved.

## 9. Oh Susannah

Foster/arr. Harvey

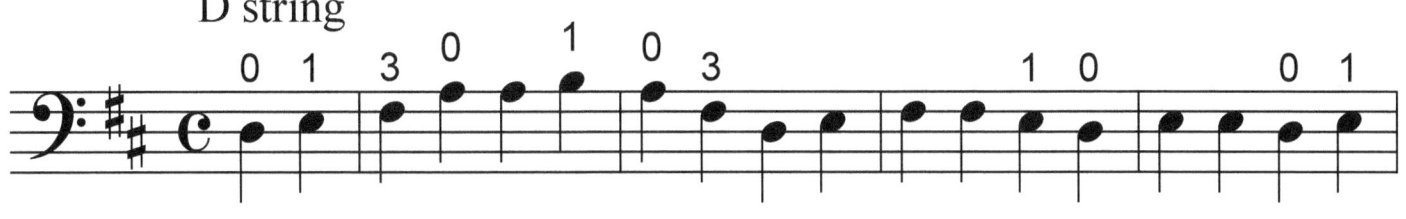
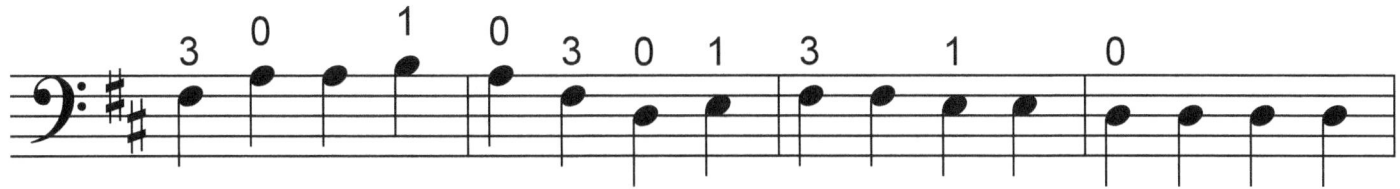

## 10. Susannah's Exercise

©2007 C. Harvey Publications All Rights Reserved.

## 11. Mountain Exercise

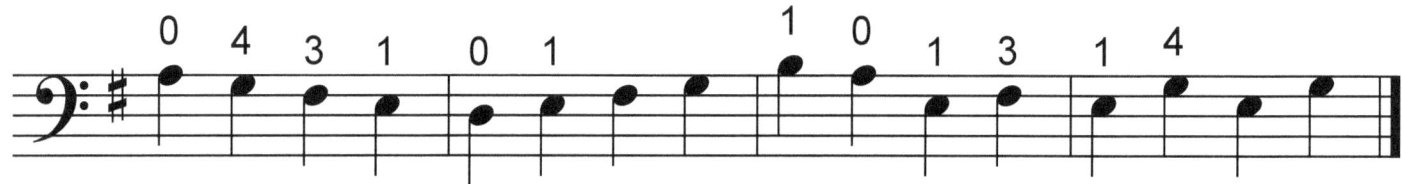

## 12. She'll Be Comin' Round the Mountain

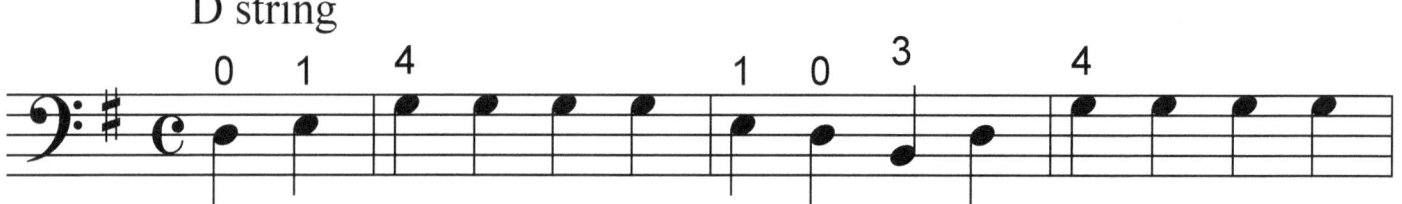

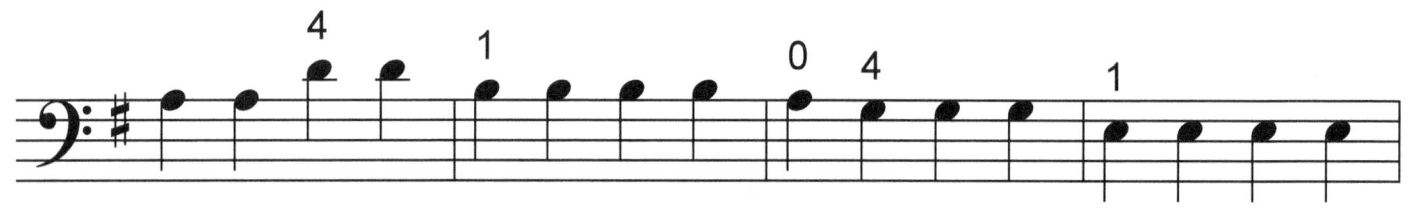

©2007 C. Harvey Publications All Rights Reserved.

## 13. Sleep Exercise

## 14. Are You Sleeping?

## 15. Sleeping Yet?

©2007 C. Harvey Publications All Rights Reserved.

## 16. Finger Trainer

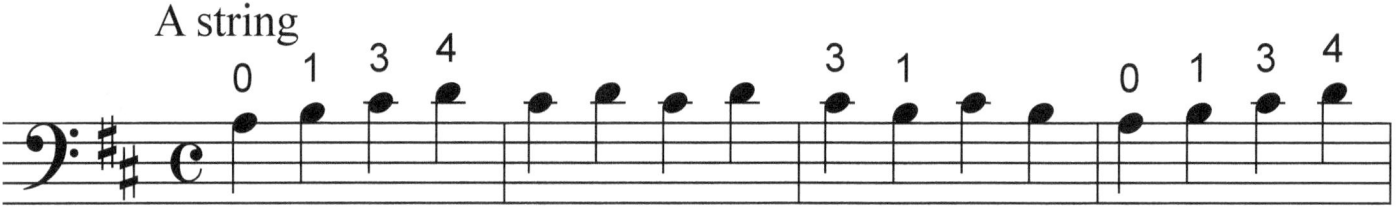
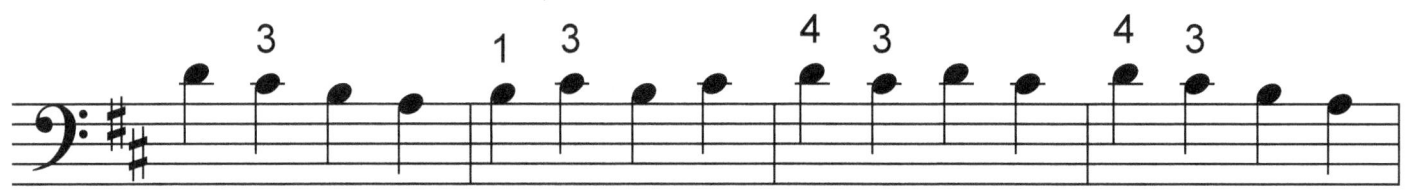

## 17. Michael, Row the Boat Ashore

## 18. Find the Hidden Songs

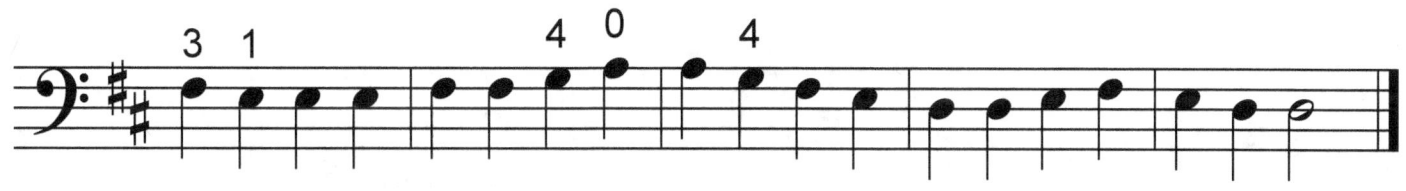

©2007 C. Harvey Publications All Rights Reserved.

## 19. Bugler's Exercise

## 20. Reveille Bugle Call

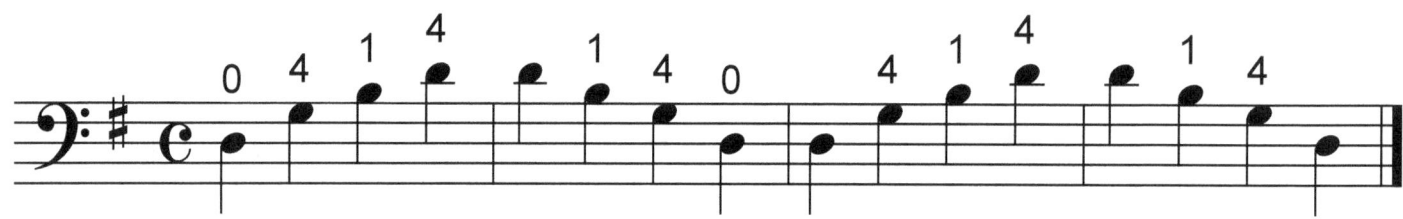

# 21. Bugler's Next Exercise

# 22. Assembly Bugle Call

# 22. Taps Bugle Call

Remember: A dotted half note gets 3 counts.

## 23. Finger Running

## 24. Swallowtail Jig

## 25. Playing on C and G

## 26. Buffalo Gals

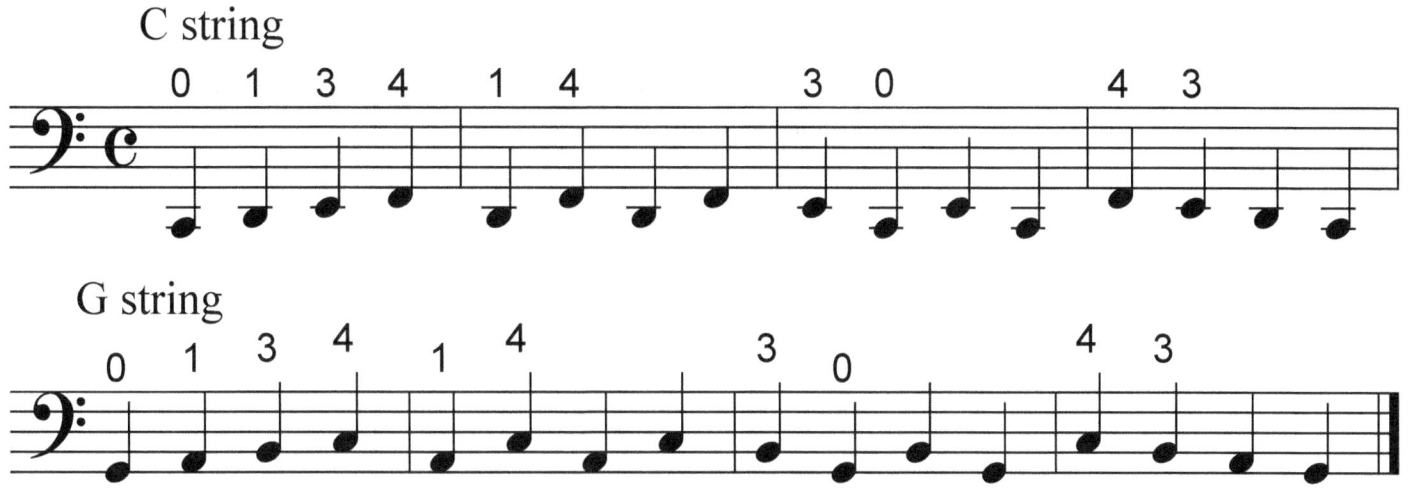

# 27. Blow the Man Down

# 28. Arpeggios

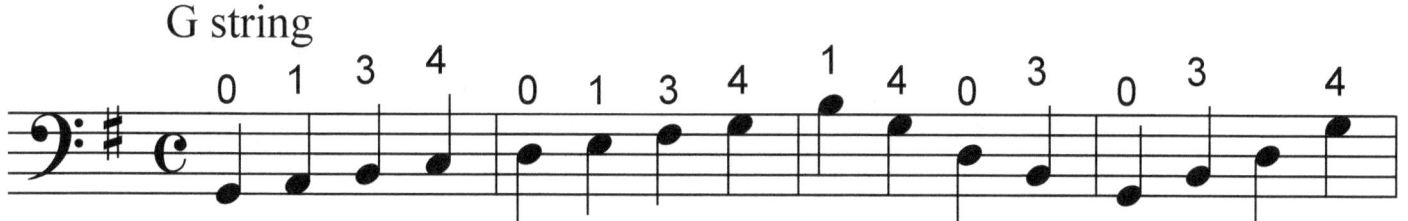
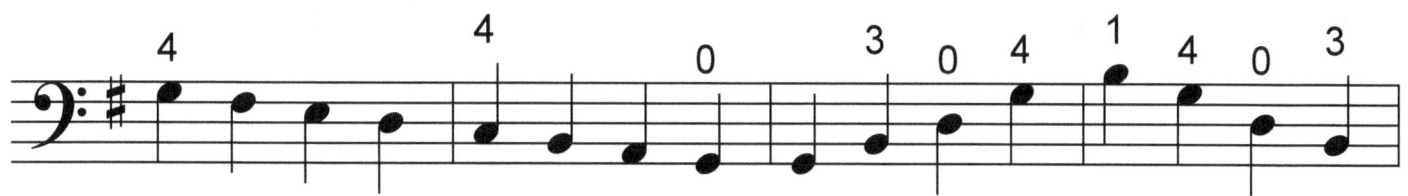

# 29. On Top of Old Smoky

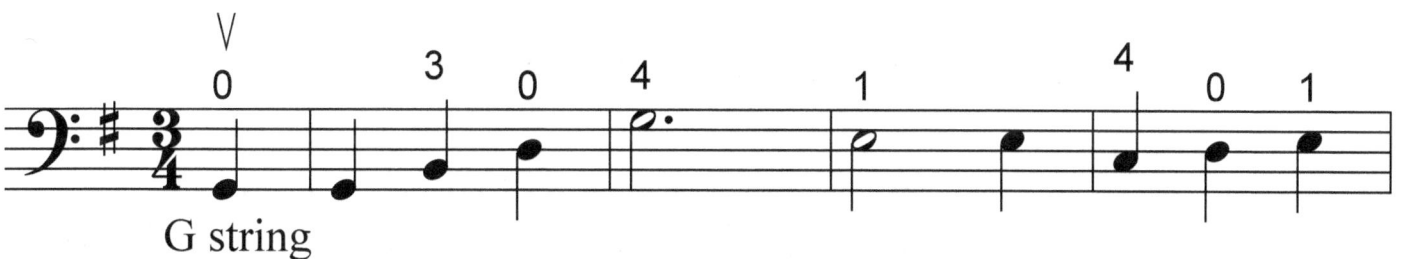

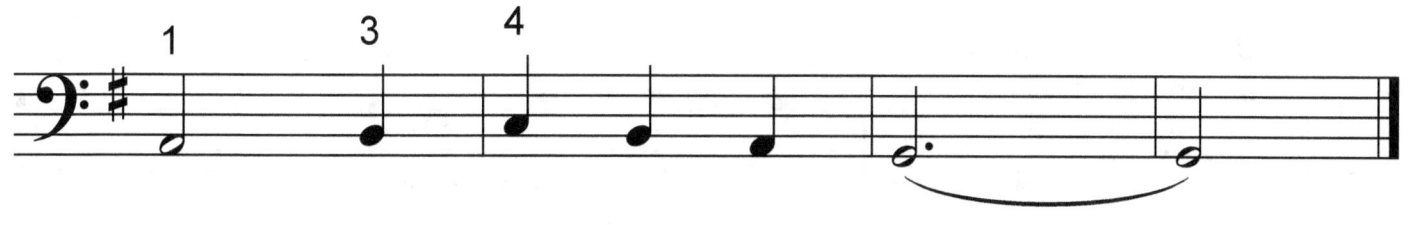

## 30. Summer Fiddle

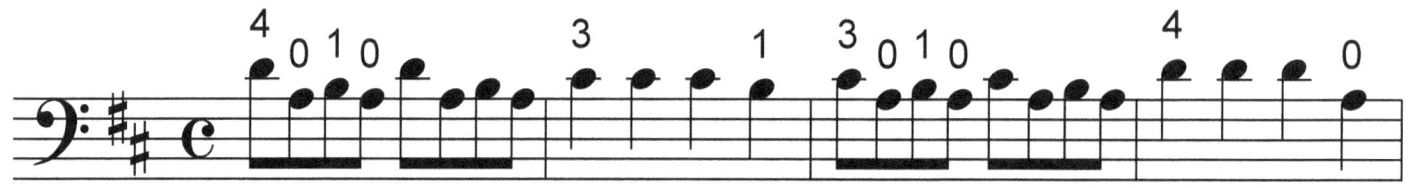
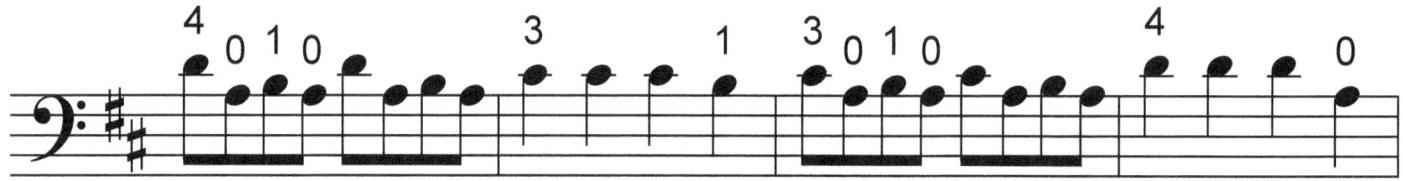

## 31. Snake Charmer's Dance

©2007 C. Harvey Publications All Rights Reserved.

## 32. This Old Man

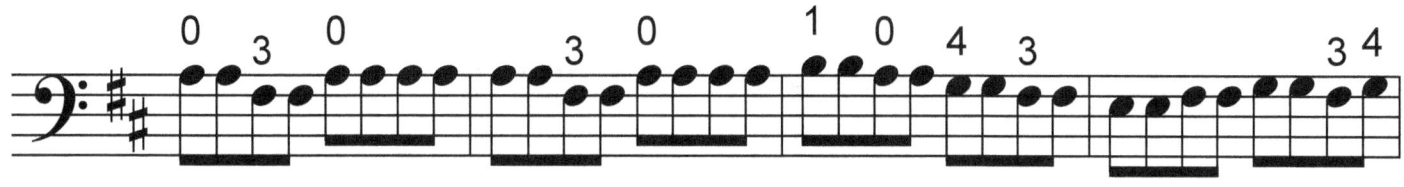
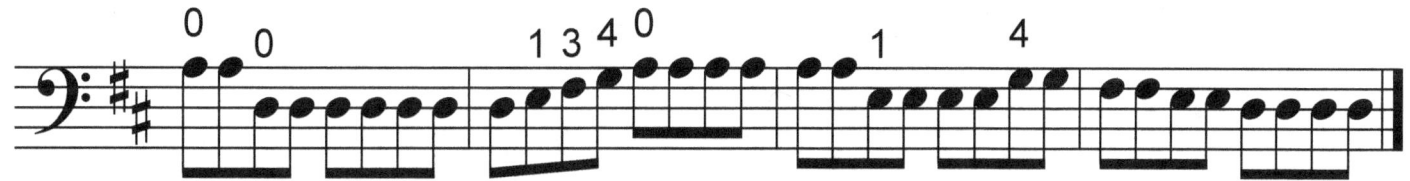

## 33. Double Trouble

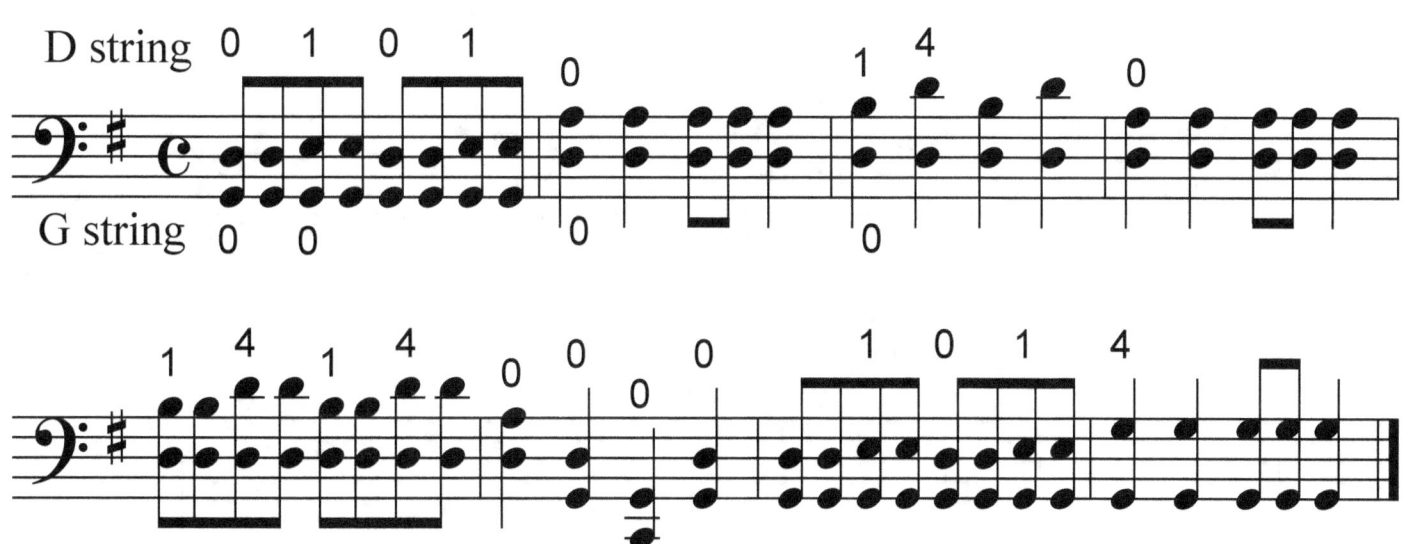

©2007 C. Harvey Publications All Rights Reserved.

## 34. String Crossing

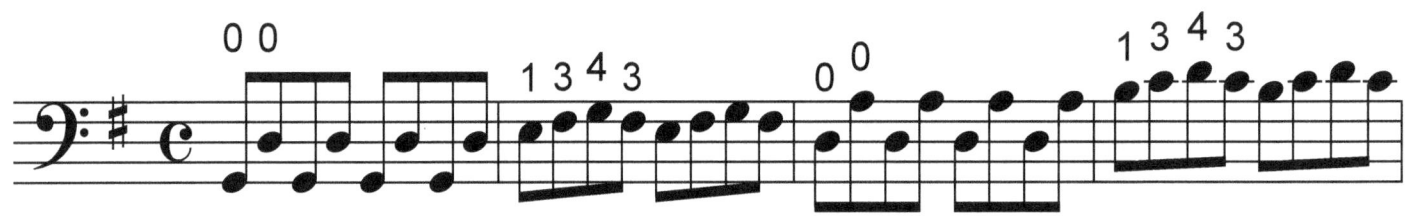

## 35. Simple Gifts

# 36. Using the 4th Finger

# 37. Battle Cry of Freedom

Root/arr. Harvey

# 40. Home on the Range

Kelley/arr. Harvey

available from **www.charveypublications.com**: CHP305

# Beginning Fiddle Duets for Two Cellos

## Cripple Creek

Trad., arr. Myanna Harvey

©2016 C. Harvey Publications All Rights Reserved.

www.ingramcontent.com/pod-product-compliance
Lightning Source LLC
Chambersburg PA
CBHW051432070526
44584CB00023B/3691